Fashions of the 40's & 50's Paper Doll Wardrobe

Lois

Kate

Lynn

the War Effort — Jennifer Steele

TUCK

Lois

Kate

1940
Janice Reed Rugee

1957
Jennifer Steele

At the onset of World War II, homefront families did their part for the war effort by participating in scrap drives. They turned in newsprint, used fats, tires, and tins. Meals were often meatless and butter-free. Ration books were needed for food and gasoline, the latter limited to three gallons a week. Women joined as volunteers in Civil Defense, drove busses and trains. "Rosie the Riveters" reported to assembly lines in war-work factories as ship builders, welders, and machine operators. In 1942, the Women's Army Auxiliary Corps (WAAC) was authorized, followed by women's corps in all other branches. These service women valiantly served as ferry pilots, plane mechanics, code clerks, and truck drivers after undergoing rigorous basic training. Their assignments released men for active duty.

1. This Signal Service WAAC uniform was proudly worn by Genevieve Szymarek. She served two enlistments during and after World War II. She was a military cryptographer, and after many assignments, finished in Washington at the Pentagon and White House code centers. Her distinguished honors include The Good Conduct Medal, American Theater Ribbon, Meritorious Unit Award, Victory Medal, and the WAAC Service Medal. Her uniform consists of a gored skirt and Eisenhower jacket of wool. The service overcoat features eight eagle-crested buttons.

2. The day after Pearl Harbor, 3,740 Red Cross chapters rallied to help win the war. They set up Blood Banks, drove ambulances and trucks, and helped at troop trains. A fine example of a Red Cross volunteer is Janice Reed Rugee who wore this uniform and donated it to the Northern Indiana Center for History collection. Jan was a South Bend native, educated at Mt. Holyoke with a degree in the then new science of Psychology. From 1941-1945 she drove trucks and ambulances for the Red Cross Motor Corps. In post-war years, Jan worked for and presided over the Junior League of South Bend, the Children's Dispensary, and the Scholarship Foundation. She also managed the bookstore at St. Mary's College, Notre Dame, Indiana.

3. On July 1, 1950, American G.I.s landed in South Korea to push back the invading North. High schoolers were forced to crouch in hallways and basements when air-raid drills became customary. Draft boards called up eligible young men, and girls often did their part for the war effort by writing to these servicemen.

The circle skirt was a must in every girl's wardrobe, usually worn with a twin sweater-set as illustrated. Heavily starched crinolines held the skirt away from the body; glued on poodles were common, giving it the name "poodle skirt." This particular one, worn by an unknown bobbysoxer, was later purchased second hand by Jan Arick, education director for the N.I.C.H. for her daughter, Jennifer Steele. Jennifer and her little pals staged imaginative back-porch dramas, self-written and directed, for the delight of their parents. Culled from the costume bag, the skirt is made of black wool felt, appliqued clock and gold chain. Pearl beads measure the hours.

1950

Genevieve Szymarek

Career Girls

Having tasted independence outside their homes during the war years, young women went out into the work force as a matter of course. "Career Girls," having been well trained at Katherine Gibbs Secretarial in New York or at the local College of Commerce, eagerly pursued work as executive secretaries or sought advancement to department store buyers, decorators, or illustrators. Some chose modeling or made executive decisions in the new field of television. Social Services and teaching were natural choices, as were airline positions. A woman could be a foreign correspondent or photo journalist. For the millions of working teenagers who babysat, clerked or car-hopped, being able to buy their own clothes became a symbol of their independence, and a brand-new retail market appeared for the "Sub-deb" set.

4a. This smart tri-tone wool gabardine suit was worn by Mrs. W.L. (Gladys) Aker. The bands of color sweep round to the middle of the back on the peplumed jacket. As a young woman, Gladys worked as bookkeeper at the South Bend Watch Factory, where she remembers Clement Studebaker as customers. She continued in that field until becoming a photo-tinter for a photography studio. She resides in Mission, Texas, but collects old newspaper clippings of her hometown, some dating from the 1800s.

4b. Seen as a luxury and investment, a fur coat was the career girl's dream. This mink-dyed squirrel belonged to Rosemary Guentert. Her stroller-length fur has padded shoulders and deep sleeves. A true career-girl, Rosemary graduated from nursing school in 1943, and served as a psychiatric and office nurse until her marriage to Edmond Ziokowski. She then reentered her profession at St. Joseph Medical Center as night supervisor, serving for 28 years and only recently retiring.

5. The black velvet and wool coat has the "New Look," a silhouette which brought excitement to women forced to wear war-time spartan and skimpy suits and blouses. With full skirts only 12 inches from the floor, and the padding shifted from shoulders to hips, Dior's designs caused a fashion revolution. The swirling coat was worn by Catherine Pfaff Cholis. A graduate of the University of Colorado in textiles, she then studied at Tobé Coburn School of Fashion Design in Manhattan. After graduation, "Kak" worked at Bloomingdales as a buyer. While modeling in one of their fashion shows, she wore this coat and bought it. Leaving New York, she received her Masters in Food at the University of Minnesota. Returning to South Bend, she settled her career as a high school teacher in that field, and married attorney Alexis Cholis. Kak was an active volunteer for the Christ Child Society and Junior League of South Bend.

6. Play Ball! Beginning in her teens, Helen Steffes was an outfielder and third-baseman in the renowned American Girls' Baseball League, starting with the Rockford Peaches in 1945, Kenosha Comets in 1947, and South Bend Blue Sox from 1948-51. She raised six children while continuing to coach gradeschool girls, and currently coaches girls 18 and up while living in Michigan. Her uniform features a short skirt, which Helen describes as "well-designed for running and throwing." The side-buttoned bodice carries the seal of South Bend.

1945
Rosemary Ziokowski

Gladys Aker—1941

1947

Catherine Pfaff Cholis

Lois

1950

Helen Steffes

Kate

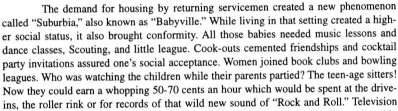

Suburbia

The demand for housing by returning servicemen created a new phenomenon called "Suburbia," also known as "Babyville." While living in that setting created a higher social status, it also brought conformity. All those babies needed music lessons and dance classes, Scouting, and little league. Cook-outs cemented friendships and cocktail party invitations assured one's social acceptance. Women joined book clubs and bowling leagues. Who was watching the children while their parents partied? The teen-age sitters! Now they could earn a whopping 50-70 cents an hour which would be spent at the drive-ins, the roller rink or for records of that wild new sound of "Rock and Roll." Television antennas rose over every roof. Daters and families gathered in front of black and white sets to watch "Your Show of Shows" on Saturday night.

7. The perfect costume for a '50s back yard barbecue is this ensemble of emerald green linen capri pants and pure silk shirt embroidered with butterflies and flower petals. It was worn by Verna Postel of Grosse Pointe, Michigan, who loved to search out estate sales where she would find designer clothes. Two of her "finds" appear on these pages. During the Depression, Verna made hats professionally and sewed for her daughters. She studied for and became a Master Gardener, fulfilling her love of all things beautiful, and was a judge for both state and national garden shows. She is shown as a true suburbanite, surrounded by children, who in truth, belong to paper doll Lynn.

8. Sheath dresses such as this yellow linen from '55 were considered a very sexy curve revealing fashion, especially when worn with spiky stiletto heels. Model Hertha Miley's sheath is trimmed with appliqued satin vines, velvet leaves and over-sized pale-yellow chrysanthemums which fall loosely away from the body. Hertha moved to the United States in 1948, traveling as a model for Daimler Benz of North America. As a model, she was registered with Chicago and South Bend agencies, traveling extensively. Many of the gowns worn promoting her prestigious clients have been donated to the N.I.C.H. collection. Presently, she lives and works in Arizona.

9. Fads of the '50s: 30 million hula-hoops sold; chlorophyll in everything, flying saucers, bomb shelters and "way-out" was in. It was cool to "hang-out," party at the beach, or go with the gang to the roller-rink. Teenagers wore short shorts, pop-it-beads, poodle cuts and the color pink. Another of Verna Postel's finds is this checked gingham playsuit. Eyelet on the ruffles and flaring pleats give it a youthful look. Watch that ice-cream cone!

1950
Verna Postel

1955
Hertha Miley

1940
Verna Postel

Charity balls and Proms

The dance craze, begun in the '20s, climaxed in the '40s and '50s. In the '40s, teenagers jitterbugged to big-band swing, or swayed to the silky sound of The Voice, Frank Sinatra. Ten years later, they were rocking to the roll of the King, Elvis Presley, and learning how to dance the Stroll while watching Dick Clark's American Bandstand.

Young married couples and oldsters formed dance clubs where ladies were assured a full dance card. Couples took ball-room, cha-cha, and mambo lessons so they never needed to leave the dance floor as orchestras alternated pop and Latin rhythms. Charitable organizations, particularly hospital boards, turned this popularity to their favor and charity balls became their major fund-raisers. Here, society matrons and shop-girls could join the conga-line while showing off their new ball-gowns and diamond or rhinestone jewels — all in the name of charity. "I Could Have Danced All Night" to the fresh new music of Lerner and Lowe and Cole Porter, Irving Berlin, and Rogers and Hammerstein. Popular dance clubs of South Bend were the Midnighters, Assemblers, and Married Folks. Teens flocked to private tea-dances, fraternal junior groups, or R.O.T.C. Balls and U.S.O. dances.

1948
Volberg Olsen

10. This Designer bronze satin ball gown once swept the floor with its full train on the bias-cut gored skirt. A draped cape forms a sleeve effect; it is hung with self-fabric ball-buttons. It was donated to the N.I.C.H. by Mrs. Kenneth (Volberg) Olsen. Vollie's husband was a prominent radiologist, and her volunteer hours were spent in the medical field. She was a past-president of the Women's Indiana State Medical Association and also active in the St. Joseph County Association, as well as Memorial Hospital of South Bend. The late '50s bronze beaded bag was purchased in Hong Kong as a gift to the author.

11. Our teenager flies off to the prom in this strapless tiered gown of organdy ruffles. Her waltz-length dress was popular in the '50s, and bare shoulders were always balanced by short or long gloves. This dress had been worn by Mary Lou Wiekamp, who, as Mrs. Dennis Schwartz, is known for her philanthropic efforts for her community. A tireless worker for the N.I.C.H., Mary Lou has also been involved with Carnival of the Arts, South Bend Symphony Show House, chaired Holiday Balls for the Junior League of South Bend, and is committed to perpetuating the good done by the League in the community.

12. High drama sparks this coordinated gown, coat, and gloves, all three designed and made by the mother/daughter team of Margaret Martin and Phyllis Whitcomb. Margaret's dress is of nylon jersey; the cap sleeves are set into smocked shoulders and the satin sash cinches the waist. The hip-length coat is reversible from green herringbone wool to wine knit, and to gild these pink and purple lilies, handmade satin gloves! Margaret Martin made all of daughter Phyllis' wardrobe, from toddler frocks to evening gowns, teaching her the art of fine sewing. How pleased I was, upon corresponding with the gown's creator, Ms. Whitcomb, to find she too had studied fashion design and shared a love of paperdolls.

1950

Mary Lou Schwartz

1940

Margaret Martin